·ANIMALS ILLUSTRATED·
Arctic Wolf

· ANIMALS ILLUSTRATED ·

Arctic Wolf

by William Flaherty • illustrated by Sean Bigham

INHABIT
MEDIA

Published by Inhabit Media Inc.
www.inhabitmedia.com

Inhabit Media Inc. (Iqaluit) P.O. Box 11125, Iqaluit, Nunavut, X0A 1H0
(Toronto) 191 Eglinton Avenue East, Suite 310, Toronto, Ontario, M4P 1K1

Design and layout copyright © 2018 Inhabit Media Inc.
Text copyright © 2018 by William Flaherty
Illustrations by Sean Bigham copyright © 2018 Inhabit Media Inc.

Editors: Neil Christopher, Kathleen Keenan
Art Director: Danny Christopher
Designer: Astrid Arijanto

We acknowledge the support of the Canada Council for the Arts for our publishing program.

This project was made possible in part by the Government of Canada.

ISBN: 978-1-77227-213-0

Printed in Canada

Library and Archives Canada Cataloguing in Publication

Flaherty, William, 1965-, author
Arctic wolf / by William Flaherty ; illustrated by Sean Bigham.

(Animals illustrated)
ISBN 978-1-77227-213-0 (hardcover)

1. Gray wolf--Arctic regions--Juvenile literature. 2. Wolves--Arctic
regions--Juvenile literature. I. Bigham, Sean, illustrator II. Title.
III. Series: Animals illustrated

QL737.C22F53 2018   j599.7730911'3   C2018-901886-0

Canadä   Canada Council   Conseil des Arts
            for the Arts   du Canada

Table of Contents

The Arctic Wolf

The Arctic wolf lives in Alaska, Northern Canada, and Greenland. Arctic wolves are a type of wolf with white fur. This fur helps them blend into the snowy Arctic landscape.

Arctic wolves are lean and tall, but they have smaller ears and shorter muzzles than grey wolves. The muzzle is the part of the wolf's face that sticks out, where its nose and mouth are.

The Arctic wolf's smaller ears and shorter muzzle help it conserve body heat during long, cold winters.

Adult Arctic wolves grow to between 3 and 6 feet (about 1 to 2 metres) long and weigh between 99 and 154 pounds (about 45 to 70 kilograms).

Let's learn more about Arctic wolves!

Range

Arctic wolves are found in Greenland and the Arctic regions of Canada and Alaska. These areas are very far north and are covered in ice and snow for most of the year. Arctic wolves are mostly found on land, but sometimes they are seen on the sea ice.

Sometimes Arctic wolves roam very far to find food. They can travel great distances in a single day.

Arctic wolves usually travel in a group called a "pack," but sometimes they are spotted on their own.

When they are trying to catch prey, Arctic wolves can run up to 40 miles (about 64 kilometres) per hour. Prey are the animals that Arctic wolves hunt and kill for food.

Skeleton

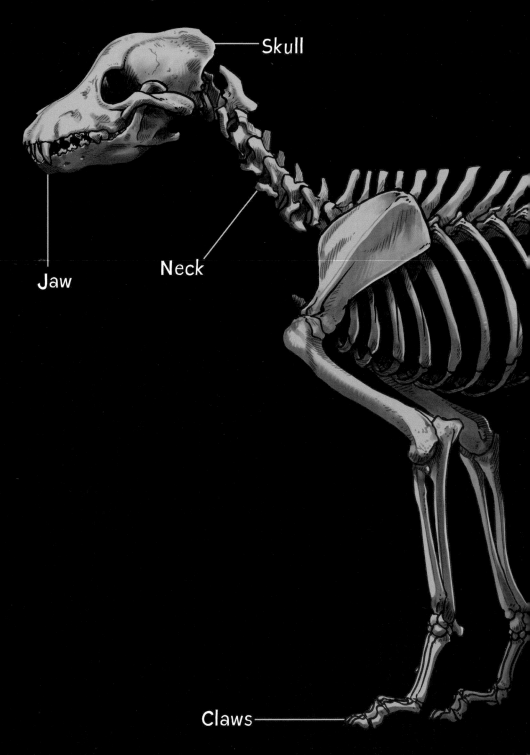

Skull

Jaw

Neck

Claws

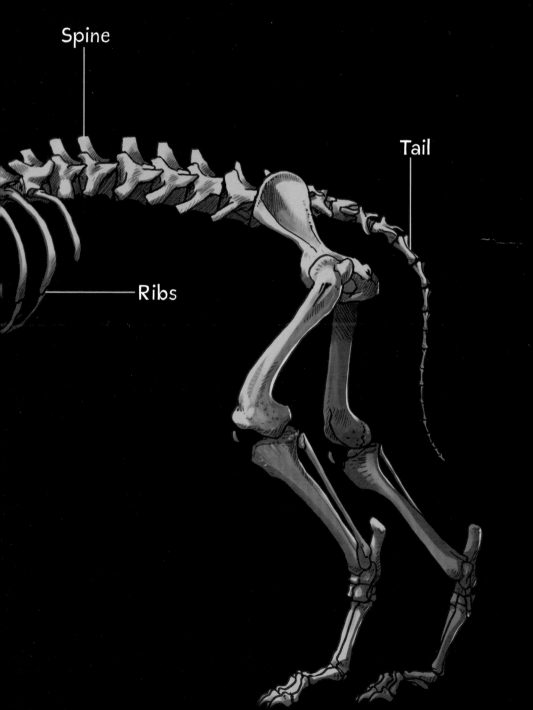

Spine

Ribs

Tail

Skull

Arctic wolves have 42 very sharp teeth that they use to kill and eat their prey. They eat every bit of their prey—even the bones!

Arctic wolves have powerful jaws, making it easy for them to tear apart flesh and bones.

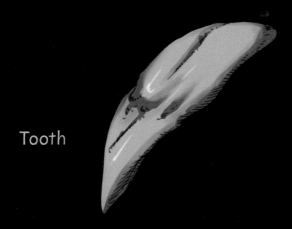

Tooth

Fur

Fur layers

With their white fur, Arctic wolves are able to blend into the ice and snow of the Arctic. They have two layers of fur that are very important for their survival. The inner layer gets thicker in winter to keep them warm. The outer layer is waterproof to keep them dry. Thanks to their fur, Arctic wolves stay warm even in the coldest temperatures.

Diet

Arctic wolves are carnivores, which means that they eat other animals. They hunt muskox, caribou, Arctic hares, and seal pups. Arctic wolves almost always hunt in packs when they're trying to catch large prey like a muskox.

Some Arctic wolves will hunt smaller prey if they can't catch a muskox or caribou. They have been seen eating lemmings, fish, birds, and even bird eggs.

Baby seal

Arctic wolves can go for weeks without food if they need to. Because food can be hard to find during the winter, they eat as much as they can at one time. An Arctic wolf can eat up to 20 pounds (about 9 kilograms) of meat at once!

Arctic hare

Babies

Baby Arctic wolves are called "pups," and a group of pups born at the same time is called a "litter." A female Arctic wolf has 1 litter a year of 2 or 3 pups.

Pups live in a small cave or space called a "den." Female Arctic wolves dig these dens before their pups are born. Arctic wolves are mammals, and all mammals feed their babies milk. The mother will feed the pups milk for the first few months. After that, the pups are able to eat meat.

The entire pack will help to raise the pups by protecting them from predators and hunting for them. Predators are animals that hunt and kill other animals.

Packs

A pack of Arctic wolves can have as many as 20 wolves. The more wolves there are in the pack, the stronger the pack is. Every pack has an alpha male and alpha female. The alpha wolves are the only ones in the pack who have pups. Most pups grow up to become pack members and will learn to hunt for the pack.

Adult wolves are sometimes accepted into new packs, but they can also be chased away if they try to join a new pack.

Each wolf pack has a "territory," an area of land where they live that they protect from other wolves. A wolf can even be killed for entering another pack's territory. Arctic wolves protect their territory so that they don't have to compete with other packs when they are hunting for food.

Communication

Arctic wolves communicate with
each other by making sounds
like barks and howls. Howling is
used during hunting and to alert
other wolves to prey or danger.
Arctic wolves also howl when
announcing their presence to
other wolf packs. Sometimes
they howl just for fun!
Howls can be heard up
to 3 miles (about 5
kilometres) away.

Arctic wolves also use their tails and bodies to communicate their standing in the pack. When wolves make their bodies tall and do not hide their tails, they are telling other wolves that they are in charge. But if wolves pull their bodies close to the ground and hide their tails between their legs, they are showing that they recognize another pack member as the leader.

Fun Facts

Arctic wolves are predators. They are not often hunted by other animals, but they are sometimes chased off by the animals they are trying to hunt. Inuit have seen muskoxen and polar bears chase away Arctic wolves.

When they are chased, wolves run in a straight line, unlike Arctic foxes, which run in a zigzag pattern to escape. Wolves can run for a very long distance before they get tired.

Arctic wolves behave differently depending on where they live and how many other wolves are in their pack. Although wolves are dangerous, Inuit have seen people feeding Arctic wolves right out of their hands. Wolves that are hungry or in a big group are said to be the most dangerous.

Wolves in Human Form

In Inuit mythology, stories tell about wolves that can shift
into human form. When they are humans, these beings
have sharp, pointed teeth. They howl and bark just like
wolves. They change into large wolves, their true form,
when they need to travel quickly or hunt prey.

William Flaherty is a conservation officer and an avid hunter who regularly volunteers with Iqaluit Search and Rescue. He is the author of *Animals Illustrated: Polar Bear*. He lives in Iqaluit, Nunavut.

Sean Bigham is a freelance illustrator and concept artist based out of Montreal, Quebec. He has done work for a range of clients from various industries, including video games and children's educational books. Sean attended the Alberta College of Art and Design, where he received a Bachelor of Design. *Animals Illustrated: Arctic Wolf* is his second book.